TRILLIUM TRAILS

written and illustrated by
Pamela A. Kopen, M.D.
with "The Hope of Trillium"
an environmental essay by
Dan F. Kopen, M.D.

Trillium Grandiflorum
(wake robin)
family Liliaceae
symbol of modest beauty

PADAKAMI PRESS
Forty Fort, PA

Trillium Trail
Ecology of the Mind and Heart

Published by Padakami Press,
a division of Padakami Enterprises,
23 Dana Street, Forty Fort, Pa. 18704

Drawings done in pen and ink, with water soluble colors.

Printed by Llewellyn & McKane, Inc.

First Edition

Published in the United States of America
10 9 8 8 7 6 5 4 3 2 1

Library of Congress Catalog Card Number
93-28228

ISBN 0-9628914-3-6

Library of Congress Cataloging-in-Publication Data
Kopen, Pamela A.
Trillium Trail
Written and Illustrated by Pamela A. Kopen
p. cm.
ISBN 0-9628914-3-6: $9.95
1. Human Ecology — Juvenile literature. I. Title
GF48.K67 1993
304.2--dc20
93-28228 CIP AC

This book may be ordered by mail from:
Padakami Press, 23 Dana Street, Forty Fort, Pa. 18704
(717) 287-3668

"Quality publications promoting
family, education & service"

to the children

One day, many years ago,
　　someone very wise
looked closely at this forest
　　through kind and caring eyes,
saw the beauty and the balance
　　from the Earth up to the skies,
and gave thanks to Mother Nature
　　for the cycles of our lives...

for the chance to be a resident
    of Nature's vast domain —
to see the changing seasons,
    to feel the sun and rain,
to smell the flower, to hear the wind,
    to taste the harvest grain,
and share with every living thing
    in this unbroken chain.

The wise one taught the children
     so that they might understand
that their destiny was not to be
     possessors of the land,
but, rather, to be caretakers,
     respectful of the Earth,..
to know that every entity
     has dignity and worth.

Every drop of water,
   every breath of air,
every ray of sunshine
   is part of what we share.
From the tallest Redwood giant
   to the smallest living cell,
all things are connected
   on this planet where we dwell.

The children saw the beauty
in all that they observed,
and for many generations
the balance was preserved.
They saw in every sunrise
a reason to rejoice,
and gave thanks for Nature's bounty
with heart, and hand, and voice.

But . . .
   this creative human spirit,
      which can manifest such joy,

is matched in equal measure
by a power to destroy . . .

and, in the name of "progress,"
we've sometimes taken
more than our share —
carelessly misusing
the water, land, and air.

Many precious species
    have been victims of this greed —
threatened with extinction
    by this all-consuming need
to conquer the environment
    at such a deadly cost
that the quality of human life
    is also being lost.

Οn this living planet
　　each component plays a role,
so harm to any sector
　　can cause change throughout the whole.
The outcome of this fateful change
　　the course of time will tell,
but when we harm the balance
　　we may harm ourselves as well.

Every flower of springtime
is a loving, silent prayer.
We must listen to the Earth
with our hearts and be aware
of the need to reawaken,
to show how much we care,
and to redirect our energies
toward healing and repair.

When we stop misusing
   our power to control,
we'll regain the ancient wisdom
   that resides within each soul;
we'll live again in harmony;
   we'll realize our worth . . .

and recapture our enchantment
with this wondrous planet
Earth.

"
. . . Alone, a daydream never can sprout wings,
nor can determination stand apart . . .
but both, together, can do wonderous things
when soul joins mind and intellect takes heart."

from "Imagination" by Pamela Kopen, 1969

Preserving environmental quality involves more than just caring. If we hope to be part of the solution to the problems of environmental degradation we must raise the level of awareness regarding challenges facing the environment. We can encourage both concern and action through serious efforts to educate ourselves about the processes which underlie the massive assault on the biosphere. We invite you to journey further along the path of knowledge of environmental concerns by reading "The Hope of Trillium."

The Hope of Trillium

OVERVIEW

We live during a critical period in the history of mankind's relationship with the Earth. From the dawn of civilization until the present century humans exhibited virtually no global influence on the environment and, therefore, had almost no strategic effect upon the environmental inheritance of future generations. This is no longer the case. Through enhanced technologies and patterns of production and consumption mankind is changing, often dramatically, the complex balances which make up the biosphere. The cumulative actions of the present generation of human beings will determine whether future generations inherit an hospitable environment.

While our understanding of man-made environmental challenges has advanced, our willingness and ability to manifest stewardship toward our surroundings has lagged. Even as we realize with increasing clarity and consensus the disastrous consequences of man-made threats to the biosphere, we are falling further behind in our ability to counterbalance the unprecedented pressures that we bring to bear on the environment. We are depleting natural resources and generating wastes to sustain means of production, transportation, and consumption to a degree that is disproportionate to the improvements in the quality of life we have come to expect. Additionally and emphatically, the unparalleled explosive growth in global population combined with great disparities in resource allocation serve both to compound and confound these issues.

There are no easy answers or quick fixes for our current problems. However, because of mankind's abilities to adapt to and effect change, there is hope for future generations. This hope lies in increasing awareness of the complex interrelatedness of these issues, internalization of concern for the concept of a sustainable biosphere, and commitment to restoration of environmental quality. For our own sake as well as the sake of our children and grandchildren, we must rearrange our priorities and reallocate our technologies toward environmental healing and repair.

PHILOSOPHIC PERSPECTIVE

Man's role on Earth, and in particular his relationship with the environment, has been a subject of philosophic inquiry throughout history. Two schools of thought have received the bulk of attention in recent discussions concerning environmental issues. One viewpoint is **"Man vs. Nature,"** a dichotomous, adversarial relationship. The other viewpoint is **"Man as part of Nature,"** an interdependent, holistic relationship.

The latter viewpoint, i.e., "Man as part of Nature," is felt to have been the generally prevailing attitude throughout history until the time of the industrial revolution with attendant advances in technology and the physical sciences. While not always viewed holistically, from the ancients through the preindustrial age man's role was recognized as being a part of and dependent upon Nature. As knowledge of the forces of Nature grew and concurrently capabilities to alter the environment were realized, mankind gained a sense of separateness from and superiority over Nature. An attitude that Man could control Nature and had ownership of the Earth gained wider acceptance, particularly in scientific, economic and political thought. Even some religious teachings contributed to this emerging version of the role of Man, and for the past two to three centuries the "Man vs. Nature" attitude prevailed. The feeling that Man held an adversarial possessive dominion over Nature helped to shape actions and attitudes toward the environment.

Until the present century, the debate over man's role with respect to Nature (possessor vs. steward) was mainly of academic interest, or at most had local consequences. Only Nature wielded forces with global implications. Today this debate has taken on strategic, worldwide consequences. We are faced with the inescapable knowledge that through pressures brought on by our means of production, transportation, and patterns of consumption combined with the overwhelming pressures of a burgeoning global population, we as a species have acquired the power to change the planet's environment at an accelerating rate and with global impact.

The pendulum has swung away from an attitude of adversarial ownership back to the realization that we are part of and dependent upon Nature. Man is only one of millions of species which share this planet in a complex, intricately balanced web of life. However, from among those millions of species only Man has emerged to achieve a critically strategic position of consequence with respect to the biosphere. Man alone has developed and deployed technologies which wreak havoc on a global scale.

The knowledge that has awakened us to the need to change our collective attitude of "business as usual" comes from the realization that damage to the environment is adversely impacting the quality of human life. For hundreds or perhaps thousands of years mankind has casually accepted the extinction of other species and the destruction of local and regional habitats. These eradications and disruptions appeared to be of no consequence to mankind, and often benefitted segments of the population. We now know that we are causing damage to human life on a global scale. We need to rearrange our priorities to preserve the quality of life which we had hoped to enhance through science and technology.

It is widely understood and accepted that we are *a part of*, and not *apart from*, Nature. Science, religion and philosophy have come to this recognition. Mankind must now bring politics, law and industry to this working understanding if we are to favorably influence the outcome of the work of environmental restitution which lies ahead.

GLOBAL CONCERNS

While there are many noteworthy environmental concerns, most of which receive local or regional attention, two strategic (global) concerns have emphasized the need for mankind to exercise stewardship over the thin veneer on the Earth which constitutes the biosphere. Both the "Greenhouse Effect" and "Ozone Holes" have become causes celebre for the marshalling of global environmental efforts. These high profile controversies have served to focus the attention of individuals and governments on the adverse effects of human activities on the environment.

The term **"greenhouse effect"** refers to a warming of the Earth's surface due to the entrapment of heat by gases in the upper atmosphere (stratosphere). As the concentrations of certain gases increase in the stratosphere, the amount of heat trapped at the Earth's surface increases. Human activity is now the largest contributor to the increasing levels of so-called greenhouse gases which include carbon dioxide, water vapor, methane, and nitrous oxide.

The greenhouse effect can be viewed as analogous to what happens to an automobile that sits in the sun with the windows closed. The sun's rays enter the windows and warm the interior. Heat results which remains trapped inside the car. In a similar fashion, the sun's rays which strike the Earth result in generation of heat, much of which is then radiated back toward space. This infrared radiation (heat) is trapped in proportion to the concentration of gases in the upper layers of the atmosphere. As more greenhouse gases accumulate, more heat is trapped. The single largest contributing gas is carbon dioxide, which is increasing at an alarming rate. This is due in large part to human activities such as the burning of fossil fuels and the depletion of large areas of the Earth's forests.

Ironically, air pollutants may counterbalance the greenhouse effect to some degree. Such contaminants in the atmosphere act to deflect a portion of the sun's incoming rays and thereby prevent some of the warming that would otherwise occur. However, it is the consensus among scientists worldwide that a gradual and accelerating warming of the environment has begun and that this will have consequences that are unfavorable to human habitation.

The complexities involved in the greenhouse effect are such that no one can predict with certainty the outcome of this change or the rate at which changes will occur. A background greenhouse warming has been present throughout the time span of human existence. This warming has allowed life as we know it to evolve. The Earth's surface would be much colder were it not for the estimated 30° to 35°C of warming due to this natural background. This is crucial to environmental water reserves, as much less water would be available in liquid form for use by living organisms at those colder temperatures. Now, however, what was a delicate global balance is threatened. Major climate changes, rising global sea levels, large areas of desertification, and increasing frequency and severity of storms are a few of the potential consequences of global warming.

The second strategic challenge, and one which many scientists feel has been more conclusively documented, is the accelerating depletion of stratospheric ozone, i.e., the production of **"ozone holes"** over large areas of the Earth's surface.

Ozone is a chemical substance closely related to oxygen. In the highest levels of the atmosphere this gas protects the Earth's surface from ultraviolet radiation. Ultraviolet rays are known to cause damage to life forms. In particular, ozone absorbs UV-B wavelengths, which have the most damaging effects on DNA in living organisms. In humans ultraviolet exposure increases the incidence of skin cancers and cataracts as well as causing depression of the immune system. However, the direct effects on humans may be a very small part of the overall impact on the biosphere. Increased levels of ultraviolet radiation may cause disastrous changes in fragile ecosystems which underlie areas of ozone depletion. For example, the possibility of destruction of plankton in the seas, which are a fundamental part of the food chain in the marine environment, could have widespread and overwhelming effects on marine life. Also, some evidence suggests that increased exposure to ultraviolet radiation renders vegetation less effective at the process of photosynthesis (the chemical process occurring in plants which acts to absorb carbon dioxide and produce oxygen) thus adding to the increasing atmospheric burden of carbon dioxide and depletion of oxygen.

Ozone itself is a harmful gas when we are exposed to it directly. In the lower levels of the atmosphere ozone is a major component of smog. It is in the upper levels of the atmosphere (stratosphere) that ozone serves to protect the biosphere, and it is in the upper levels where ozone is being depleted at an accelerating rate. This depletion is caused by the upward migration of gases produced by human activity some of which react chemically to destroy ozone molecules in the stratosphere. The major offending gases are chloroflurocarbons (CFCs) which have been in widespread use in industry and households. Many other upwardly migrating pollutants also play a role in destroying this protective layer of ozone, including bromine containing flurocarbons, also referred to as halons.

"Ozone holes" are areas of significant reduction in the ozone layer. These "holes" appear in cycles and have occurred mainly over the poles, with the South Pole having sustained the major impact to date. It is thought that the polar regions are more susceptible to this occurrence because of the colder temperatures which allow the formation of stratospheric clouds made up of ice crystals. These ice crystals do not form to the same extent over warmer areas of the planet, and they serve as a surface upon which the chemical reactions which deplete ozone can take place. The availability of a surface for chemical reactions increases tremendously the efficiency of ozone-destroying gases. There has also been recent documentation of significant ozone depletion over more temperate regions of the Earth, which include the land masses where the bulk of humanity resides. This depletion is less readily explained by current understanding, but is causing heightened concern in the global scientific community.

These two strategic challenges have served to focus worldwide attention on the environmental debate. There are numerous other pressures which we are placing on the environment. Most of these have a more regional or local focus, but all may, through the complex web of interconnectedness, impact on a global scale.

Selected Environmental Concerns: "Sand Drops"

AIR

Air pollution is a widely recognized problem that has always plagued industrialized urban areas. The most widely recognized form of air pollution, **smog,** (a mixture of contaminants such as ozone, nitrous oxides, and sulfur particles) is produced in largest part by industrial activity and transportation. The effects of smog on human health are well documented. There are many urban areas where the quality of the air is increasingly unfit for human exposure. Smog alerts are a way of life in some large cities and serious respiratory illnesses and deaths have been attributed to this problem.

The erosion of the quality of air we breathe serves as a poignant reminder of the effects of human activity on the biosphere and of our intricate interconnectedness with the environment. Every time we take a deep breath of air, we inhale in excess of a million trillion molecules of oxygen. That same oxygen has been present throughout human history and predated the appearance of human beings by more than a billion years. Among those countless trillions of molecules that we inhale are oxygen atoms that are shared with all life forms on this planet. The very same oxygen atoms that are inhaled by us on a daily basis have been inhaled by the gamut of human beings throughout history, famous and infamous, rich and poor, good and bad, and the nameless hordes of humanity. This understanding of our interdependence upon the same shared oxygen throughout the biosphere is articulated in the Eastern concept of "Budda's Breath;" and just as we share oxygen, all the physical elements which combine to constitute the human body are comprised of similarly shared atomic and molecular resources.

Acid rain is another form of pollution which results from human activity. Sulfur dioxides and nitrous oxides are the major components. These are placed into the atmosphere largely through industrial and utility smokestacks. These particles migrate and subsequently precipitate in the form of rain and snow over widespread areas often remote from their sources. The effects may be profound on lakes and forests sometimes hundreds or even thousands of miles from the sources of the pollution. Several lakes and forests are dead or dying because of the acidity which has been rained upon them, no longer habitable by many of the indigenous species, both plant and animal. We are also witnessing the destruction of statues and monuments that have withstood weathering over hundreds or even thousands of years, only to crumble and decay in the face of air pollution during the past few decades. Such adverse effects are dramatic reminders of the insidious impact that human activity can have on the environment. A causal relationship is often unsuspected because the effects are removed in time and place from the origin of the pollutants.

Globally, we are adding **carbon dioxide** to the atmosphere at a rate unparalleled in history. Over the past century the average level of carbon dioxide in the atmosphere has risen by roughly 30% (about 80 ppm). The biosphere experiences yearly cycles of carbon dioxide concentrations with relatively small (5-10 ppm) differences in the peak and trough levels. The lowest concentrations of carbon dioxide correspond to summer in the Northern hemisphere and the highest concentrations occur during the winter of the Northern hemisphere. The oceans and the forests serve as reciprocal "lungs" of the Earth, acting to consume carbon dioxide and to produce oxygen, (whereas animal lungs take in oxygen and give off carbon dioxide). It is thought that the yearly variations in carbon dioxide levels are due mainly to the changes in foilage over the large land masses covered by forests in the Northern hemisphere. These forests are more effective in consuming carbon dioxide during the summer. We have yet to determine the full effects that this relentless rise in the overall carbon dioxide content of the atmosphere will have on life forms. The greenhouse effect is the most discussed consequence of this change, but it is likely many other changes are also occurring.

It should be further understood that atmospheric carbon dioxide is in a complex state of dynamic equilibrium with carbon dioxide in the oceans. In fact, over 98% of the total atmospheric/oceanic carbon is held in the oceans. Serving as repositories, the Earth's oceans and seas play an extremely important role in reducing the concentrations of carbon dioxide in the atmosphere. Both physical (solubility) and biologic (phytoplankton) sumps act to remove carbon dioxide from the air. In a very real sense the oceans and seas serve as a large buffering crucible for man-made (anthropogenic) carbon dioxide. While the oceans are not able to fully compensate for the dramatic increases in carbon dioxide resulting from human activities, were it not for the complex interactions of atmospheric carbon dioxide with the oceanic sumps, the concentrations of carbon dioxide in the air would likely be two to three times the current rapidly rising levels.

The complexity of this equilibrium is further impacted by increased rates of photosynthesis occurring in most terrestrial plant species at higher concentrations of carbon dioxide. This serves to offset in part man-made increases in carbon dioxide. However, ongoing destruction of large areas of forested land will result in a decrease in the effectiveness of this element of the buffering equation.

The overall effect of human activities in the biosphere is a complex ongoing acid-base experiment on a global scale, the consequences of which we are only beginning to comprehend.

WATER

Water quality concerns are a daily fare in the global media. In some areas of the world water quality problems are the major source of disease and death among large segments of the population. Both inadequate supplies and impure freshwater sources threaten the quality of life in many nations.

Freshwater constitutes only about 2½% of total water in the biosphere. Of the freshwater used by mankind approximately three-fourths is used to irrigate croplands. In the United States it is estimated that approximately 40% of freshwater is used for irrigation with industry and utilities using another 50%. Only 10% of freshwater use is attributable to household consumption.

Overuse and **pollution** of our freshwater resources has become rampant. In the area of agriculture, inefficiencies and misapplications along with the use of fertilizers, herbicides, and pesticides have resulted in problems over large areas of watershed. One example is the process of **eutrophication** of lakes and reservoirs. This results from the overgrowth of algae as a result of the presence of chemical pollutants, mainly phosphates, which promote their growth. The algae then deplete the oxygen reserves in the water and render lakes and reservoirs uninhabitable to many species of aquatic life.

Increasingly, there are instances where water quality has been threatened to the point that consumption of water is deadly. This can result from the overgrowth of bacteria from human as well as animal wastes in sewage, and also through increasing concentrations of **toxic trace metals.** Such metals are part of some finished products. Additionally, metals can be leached from natural repositories in the soil through irrigation, or appear in the effluent from industrial production and storage sites, ultimately finding their way into lakes and reservoirs.

Heavy metals are a group of fifteen atomic substances which constitute the densest of the metallic elements. Biologic organisms require trace amounts of some of these metals such as copper, molybdenum, and zinc for normal life processes. Others of these metals are not essential to life, but can be quite harmful, some at exceedingly low concentrations. The most toxic include arsenic, thallium, mercury, cadmium, antimony, and lead. These metals act to disrupt the biochemistry of cells by interacting with chemical substances in the body which are vital to life processes. Even those metals required for life in trace amounts can be harmful when present in excess.

Exposure to heavy metals has increased steadily since the industrial revolution and dangerously high levels exist in some areas, including some surface and ground water reservoirs. One of the unexpected effects of the use of sludge from municipal sewage facilities as a recycled fertilizer product is the potential increased uptake by crops of heavy metals contained in the sludge. These heavy metals then become part of the food chain and the ultimate result may be increased human exposure to these harmful substances. The process of **biologic concentration** describes the increasing concentrations of these elements as they circulate through the biosphere, later to be even further concentrated through a process described as **food chain magnification.** Some heavy metals are also released into the atmosphere in gaseous form as by-products of industrial technologies. Even the rather basic technology of hands-on mercury use as an agent to bind gold in gold mining in the Amazon is causing the release of hundreds of tons of this element into the atmosphere and watershed yearly. Additionally, some pesticides have contained heavy metals (e.g., thallium) as a deliberate attempt to utilize their toxic properties. The net effect of human activity has been increased exposure to heavy metals by life forms throughout the biosphere. Various of these substances, including other toxic trace metals, have been associated with increased incidences of cancers, respiratory diseases, cardiac and nervous system illnesses, and birth defects.

While there have been isolated instances where water quality has improved in rivers and lakes as a result of intensive efforts to eliminate and manage pollutants, worldwide we are witnessing a devastating attack on the Earth's freshwater resources. Even at the proportionately small level of direct human consumption, we have seen debates rage over the risks and benefits of water treatments such as chlorination and fluorination each of which admittedly have had both beneficial as well as harmful effects on consumers.

While much attention has been paid to what individuals and households can do to preserve freshwater resources, the greatest users of freshwater are agriculture and industry, which together dwarf household use by a factor of about 10 to 1. Clearly, when it comes to freshwater, the solution to pollution does not lie in the home. This is not to diminish the importance of husbanding this resource across the entire spectrum of human use, but only to point out where the greatest leverage for improvement in quality exists, namely in corporate boardrooms and governmental chambers. This principle of leveraged attention in government and industry holds true for virtually all environmental threats.

Over 97% of the Earth's water is in the form of saltwater. The quality of the Earth's **marine environment** is also deteriorating. The high profile reports of medical and industrial wastes and oil spills washing up on shores are simply the tip of an iceberg of pollution. The magnitude to which we have polluted the Earth's oceans and seas is not known, but it is likely to be far greater than imagined. Much of this pollution has been unregulated and is not accessible to evaluation as it is for the most part out of sight. Using the seas as a convenient dumping ground for wastes of all kinds has a long history. This abuse of the oceans, including the widespread deliberate and sometimes accidental dumping of tremendous quantities of wastes, including hazardous and nuclear wastes, has occurred largely outside the realm of public awareness. The recently noted phenomenon of **bleaching of coral reefs** is thought by many to be an indicator of very serious changes in the marine environment. This phenomenon may portend an environmental disaster of great magnitude and global consequence unfolding in the depths of our oceans.

LAND

Human use and abuse of the land is increasing worldwide. The fertile soils of our planet are being laid waste at an unsustainable rate. Through activities such as deforestation and poor agricultural management we are laying bare topsoils and witnessing the loss of a significant percent of our arable land on a yearly basis. **Overgrazing** and **improper crop rotation** have also contributed to the conversion of large areas of what was once rich and fertile topsoil to at best marginal agricultural areas and in some cases, areas that are unfit for agriculture. **Inappropriate irrigation** can also result in **salinization** of land areas. Increased salinity of soil can result as a by-product of irrigation and evaporation. Such land no longer sustains agriculture. The salt content of the soil in such areas has increased to levels that can no longer support crop growth.

Issues in land use can be extremely complex as witnessed in our Pacific Northwest where we have to consider not only the health of forest vis-a-vis lumbering interests, but also the health of freshwater and fishing interests which are intricately interconnected with the interests of those who timber. Additionally, the health of human communities and well-being of families is often dependent upon human interaction with the resources of the forests and freshwaters. The spotted owl has come to symbolize and may serve as the species which helps to crystallize the debate over opinions ranging from overuse, sustainable use, or no direct use at all.

Deforestation of huge tracts of tropical rain forests has attracted increasing attention. It is widely understood that this poses a threat to the global environment. Tropical rain forests are being destroyed at a rate exceeding 40 million acres per year. This is particularly destructive of the nutrients contained in these areas as most rain forests hold the bulk of their nutrients in the forest canopy, whereas in temperate forests most of the nutrients reside in the soil. The result of deforestation in tropical areas is to expose a relatively poor soil to rapid erosion and to interrupt an important part of the water cycle over large areas, as tropical rain forests are integral to the evaporation/precipitation cycles in the tropics. However, it is not enough for industrialized nations to admonish third world nations to halt this process. Those nations are simply mimicking many developed nations which long ago depleted their virgin forests for agricultural and industrial development.

Desertification is turning once fertile areas suitable for human habitation into arid wastelands. This is occurring on a large scale in several areas of the globe as a result of misuse and overuse of land. **Wetlands destruction** is occurring throughout the globe. These areas have provided a natural habitat to many species and also serve as buffer zones for the effects of human activity. Many wetlands have been stressed to the point that their buffering capacities have been overwhelmed. These important protective reserves have been damaged and in some instances completely destroyed by pollution and site development.

WASTES

Our concept of waste needs to be redefined. Traditional views vastly underestimate the amount of waste associated with things we use on a daily basis. If we analyze what happens with consumer goods it becomes apparent that inordinate amounts of waste are generated in the production and distribution of common items. Every article which is produced results in the production of a roughly equal bulk of waste material at the production site; it is then often packaged in materials which result in waste at the site of packaging production and which then become waste as the packaging is disposed of; and ultimately the object itself becomes waste when it is discarded. This is a form of **triple jeopardy** that the biosphere is exposed to for the sake of convenient human consumption. The energy requirements of such production and packaging processes are also a source of significant consumption of natural resources, further compounding the waste associated with consumer goods.

Hazardous wastes are afforded a separate classification because of their more immediate threat to human well-being. The chemical industry, which has given us a continuing array of products that enhance the quality of life for individuals, is a major producer of hazardous wastes. It is estimated that of the few million chemical compounds created by man, in excess of 80,000 find deployment in industry. **Chlorinated organic chemical compounds** constitute a group of some fifteen thousand of these chemicals which have been manufactured and are used throughout the range of human activities. These chlorinated hydrocarbons include not only substances recognized as dangerous such as dioxans, PCBs and some pesticides, but also many other products such as polyvinyl chlorides (PVCs), chemicals used in the medical field, and common industrial chemicals. Some of these substances have long half-lives and are ubiquitous in their distribution, being recoverable from the tissues of living species from all areas of the globe.

Increasingly, there is a concern that these chemicals may be contributing to some disturbing trends in human health. Circumstantial evidence links some organochlorines to increased rates of cancer and also to reproductive system defects, particularly in males. There is some speculation that these chemicals, even in trace amounts, may have harmful effects that can skip the generation directly exposed to the substances, and then impact on the offspring of the exposed individuals and animals. There is an ongoing debate in the scientific and industrial community regarding the use of chlorinated organic compounds. As with many individual instances of environmental concern, the exact nature of the deleterious effects of these chemicals has not been conclusively established. On the basis of what is known and suspected, there is growing scientific and industrial concern calling for a phase-out of chlorine and chlorinated hydrocarbons, and for substituting environmentally benign technologies and substances. Overall, it is believed that the concentration of chlorine in the air we breathe has increased by over 500% in the past 50 years in what many believe is a generalized **chlorination** of the biosphere. We have yet to understand the impact of this process.

Nuclear wastes, the results of both nuclear power generation and of nuclear weapons production, include some materials which will remain hazardous for thousands of years and require tremendous resources to store. We have yet to devise safe and effective means for storing these wastes, particularly high level nuclear wastes. Nor have we developed acceptable means of destroying them. Under some of our nation's nuclear weapons facilities areas ranging up to 200 square miles have been reported to be polluted with unacceptably high concentrations of radioactivity in the ground water. Also, tremendous stores of **conventional** and **biological weapons** exist in areas throughout the world. The sites of production and storage of these materials, which number in the thousands worldwide, present toxic and hazardous considerations ranging from undetonated explosives and biologic and chemical weapons cannisters to an array of hazardous compounds in the soil and water. We are just beginning to become aware of the need to address these issues, including the politically sensitive aspects of this class of pollutants, which include the classified nature of this information, and the attendant litigation potential among former employees and neighbors of these facilities.

Nonbiodegradabiltity of many of our products, particularly plastics, presents a problem since permanent storage or destruction must be developed for this increasingly problematic bulk of materials. The spector of mammals dying through entanglement in discarded plastics and the discovery of these throw away articles in the intestines and stomachs of marine life only serve to underscore the widespread areas that are affected by human wastes. No area of the Earth is free from these materials.

Paper processing plants also serve as major sources of difficult pollution problems, and consume huge numbers of trees. Paper and paper products constitute a large proportion of solid wastes in landfills, and are the single largest bulk contributor to most landfills. This space is increasingly expensive and difficult to come by. While recycling sounds like an obvious answer to the problems of paper production, the recycling processes themselves, while improved in recent years, generate hazardous wastes. Furthermore, recycled paper often constitutes a relatively small proportion of some of the paper and paper products which are labeled as recycled. While the concept of recycling has an attraction, the practice is not without its harmful side effects. The paper processing industry also employs huge amounts of chlorinated chemicals, and contributes to the general problems of chlorination. New processes which are not chlorine dependent are finding some deployment.

One particularly invisible environmental threat that technology brings increasingly to bear on large numbers of people is the energy of **electromagnetic fields** (EMFs). Once regarded as eccentrics and alarmists, scientists who warned of the hazards of EMF exposure have been vindicated through studies that link high levels of such exposure to increased incidences of childhood leukemia. There are those who feel that much more is at stake in terms of human health when dealing with the electric and magnetic fields generated by power sources such as power lines and power stations, electric appliances (TVs, microwave ovens, electric blankets, etc.) and the broad range of exposure to signals transmitted throughout the globe. We are just beginning to understand the effects of such exposures. The effects on human health are not immediately apparent and exposure is often not even suspected, rendering a causal relationship difficult to recognize and establish. The litigation potential of such exposure is so overwhelming that disclosure of the effects carries risks that render accurate appraisals difficult if not impossible. Additionally, there is a natural background of electromagnetic radiation which needs to be considered in any assessment of the effects of these energy fields.

What we are witness to is a full-scale assault on land, water, and air as these inanimate resources are being used and abused in a manner and to a degree not seen in history. There are, in addition, other serious threats to the biosphere. Formidable challenges to life forms with which we share the planet may be no less consequential to the quality of human life than are threats to the inanimate resources of the environment.

SPECIES CHALLENGES

Some of the most heartfelt effects of environmental distress come in the form of **species extinctions,** particularly of mammalian and avian species. It is also the threat of species extinction that sometimes gives rise to the most vitriolic rhetoric between those who seek to preserve natural habitats in their pristine form and those who seek to allow commercial or residential activity in those same areas.

It has been estimated that a few hundred species of native American plants and animals have become extinct in the past two centuries. Species extinction worldwide is occurring at an accelerating rate. There is no simple solution to the problems of species preservation. All of the burdens on the environment discussed above impact in some way and to varying degrees upon the species we seek to protect. In addition to the complexities of interaction among these environmental changes, the need to consider human activities, ranging from local and regional economic development to residential and recreational opportunities, further complicates this issue.

Overfishing and whale hunting are two areas of public concern in which some progress has been made on an intermittent basis to preserve the balance of nature. While it is clear that neither fish nor whales constitute an unlimited resource, it is not clear how the nations of the world can assure the preservation of these species in the face of decidedly different national interests in harvesting such shared resources. These areas of concern serve to point out the inadequacy of current economic and political mechanisms in safeguarding a shared global reserve such as the sea.

While threats to large mammals and birds are the most visible and evocative of the species challenges, lesser known but certainly no less important species (genetic) pressures exist. The dangers of **genetic erosion** and the **loss of genetic diversity** among plants as well as animals constitute major concerns.

This century has witnessed an increasing reliance upon fewer species of food crops as sources of nutrition for mankind. In addition, in the search for higher yields per acre, we are reducing the number of genetic strains of each species of food crop under cultivation. This increasing reliance on single or reduced numbers of genetic strains of fewer species of food crops has resulted in a narrowing of the range of biologic diversity among plants which are accepted as food staples in the world. This is referred to as a trend toward **monoculture agriculture.** When a threat appears in the form of a new predator or disease, it becomes a much more profound challenge than it would have been under the circumstances of greater natural genetic diversity among these crops. The so-called "Vavilovian Centers," those areas in the world from which the major food crops derive and which contain the natural genetic reserves of these crops, are under increasing residential and commercial pressures. The result has been a diminution of the natural reserves of genetic diversity among food crops. As a safeguard, large seed banks have been established in various locations, but even these from time to time are threatened by natural and political forces, and these are increasingly controlled by commercial interests.

Just as we are observing decreased natural genetic diversity among food crops, some animal species have been reduced to such small numbers that little genetic diversity exists to insure survival against threats of disease or habitat destruction. Changes in the conceptual framework of zoos include efforts to maintain genetic diversity among threatened species through breeding programs and to provide a more natural environment for zoo animals. This may be too little too late for some species, but it demonstrates an acknowledgement of the underlying problems and an attempt to respond to the threats of human pressures on natural habitats and species survival.

The well-documented disappearance of amphibian species, particularly frogs, from diverse areas of the globe, is thought to be a harbinger of the seriousness of environmental decay. For reasons that are not entirely clear, a widespread phenomenon of **amphibian disappearance** has been observed and reported. These species may be to the environment what the canary was to the underground coal miner (a harbinger of dangerous deterioration of the environment) and their disappearance may signal imminent danger and environmental decay.

It is also felt that the current massive destruction of our world's **tropical rain forests** represents a threat to species survival that far surpasses any previous species extinctions in human history. Tropical rain forests are thought to contain more species of plant and animal life than any other area in the biosphere. It is widely believed that the number of species which exist in these forests and which have yet to be identified far exceeds the number of species of life forms that have been identified to date worldwide. It is possible that we will lose genetic material of tremendous potential benefit to mankind through the destruction of this habitat and the as yet unidentified species contained therein.

The explosion of knowledge in the fields of biotechnology and genetic engineering renders an accurate appraisal of what the next century holds in regard to genetic diversity nearly impossible. Biotechnology by the turn of the century may be a $50 billion per year industry. The **Human Genome Project** is likely to have effects as profound as any technologic development in history. This worldwide collaborative effort seeks to map out the entire and exact sequence of base pairs that constitute the genetic code of humans. The potential which this knowledge will unleash will dwarf all preceding knowledge in the biologic sciences. How we will harness this potential, and if in fact we can harness this knowledge, may be the major challenge of the 21st Century. Biotechnologists and bioethicists are charged with translating this knowledge into human activity. No technology has zero risk and we should heed the lessons of history. As a rule, when the potential of a technology increases, both the potential for good as well as the potential for harm increase. Also, environmentally sound judgment almost always lags behind technologic deployment. Furthermore, no technology ever developed by man has failed to find its way into war and weapons deployment. Why should biotechnology and genetic engineering be different in this respect. These are some of the critical ethical challenges that the biosciences should be confronting as we are letting this genie out of the jar.

In summary, the net effect of human activity both in terms of the more obvious destruction of natural habitats and hunting of selected species, and also through the trend toward monoculture agriculture is serving to deplete the biosphere's reserve of genetic diversity. The long-term effect of this on human life is yet to be determined, but the consensus of opinion is that the net effect cannot be good. There are those who feel that an answer to this problem may lie in genetic engineering and biotechnology. The history of new technologies teaches us that in the long run, disadvantages often outweigh advantages, and we are most certainly going to see the fields of ethics, politics, and law lag behind the deployment of technology of this field. Once again the biosphere will be at the mercy of the deployers of technology.

POPULATION PRESSURES: THE OVERARCHING CONCERN

As serious as all the problems that have been discussed are, the impact of these activities will be intensified by the overarching pressures of **population growth.** Both the sheer numbers and the accelerating rate of growth of human population have had no historical precedent. The biomass of humanity is increasing at a rate which is unsustainable and accelerating. Early in this century there were approximately 1.5 billion people alive on our planet. Today that number is estimated to be 5.5 billion and headed towards 10 billion within the next half century. There are currently over 250 million tons of people walking the face of this globe. While this number is growing at an unsustainable rate, it also implies roughly similar tonnages of both solid and liquid human biologic wastes produced at an accelerating rate on an annual

basis. Large as these numbers are, they pale in comparison to the wastes that are generated by human activity in the industrial, agricultural, and transportational realms, where collective decisions must govern waste generation and management, and where population pressures render decision-making much more difficult.

Large areas of the globe are inhabited by people who live longer, more productive lives than at any time in history. This is in large part due to the very technologies responsible for the environmental challenges that we face. However, we have reached a time when gains in longevity and productivity are coming at disproportionate costs to the hospitable environment. Furthermore, these trends will likely be reversed in the next decade. One only needs to look at the current AIDS crisis which will soon begin to reverse this century's steady progression of increasing longevity in most nations. It is likely that within the next ten years we will see measurable decreases in the average length of life in many nations as this disease continues its inexorable march through humankind. Part of the legacy of population pressures combined with environmental decay will be the emergence of new viral and bacterial diseases as well as the re-emergence of resistant strains of old infectious diseases.

An answer to the challenge of the unsustainable growth in population is requisite to answering the environmental challenge. While some argue that an encouraging trend toward slow or no-growth is emerging in industrialized nations, given the global demographic picture we are unlikely to arrive at amicable self-regulation anytime soon. It is most likely that a combination of natural forces (including diseases), environmental degradation, and perhaps warfare, will impose a solution i.e., population control, upon us before the end of the next century.

THE ADVERSARIAL LINEAR PARADIGM

Significant disagreements exist regarding the details of specific environmental challenges we face, particularly when these challenges are taken out of the context of the complex interdependency within which they arise. However, there is general agreement that human activity has placed, and will continue at an accelerating rate to place, unprecedented challenges on our environment. The challenges that mankind has placed on the environment constitute threats to the quality of life for human beings and many of the species with which we co-inhabit the Earth. Laments that we are destroying the Earth are overstatements. What we are in the process of doing is upsetting the balances in nature which render the Earth a suitable environment for human habitation. The Earth itself will survive humankind and present life forms as it has survived countless other life forms over billions of years.

There is not much disagreement today that mankind's role in the biosphere should be one of **"stewardship,"** recognizing the responsibilities which we assume as a species toward the environment and towards each other. It is also generally recognized that there is no governmental system past or present which has not contributed to erosion of the hospitable biosphere. As bad as things have been in portions of our nation and throughout the globe as a result of our form of government and technologies, one only needs to look to Eastern Europe, Asia, and Africa to see that the answers to the problems we face in the environmental arena do not lie in any existing political program, nor are ecologic threats particular to any political system or technology.

All forms of government have failed the environment. This is probably less a reflection of the specifics of any form of government and more a reflection of the nature of human beings. The shortsightedness and self-centeredness of our approach to problems is a reflection of a process called **adversarial linear thinking.**

Adversarial linear thinking describes a paradigm that depicts the way in which most of our thoughts are framed. Based on both an assumed duality of interests between oneself and others, (or between man and the environment) and on a zero-sum mentality, this mode of thought can be understood as a mental model that attempts to simplify situations and point to solutions that are beneficial to one party in an encounter. The focus is on an "either I win or you win" adversarial mentality with consideration limited to the immediacy of the situation, both in time and place, i.e. a linear analysis. Adversarial linear thinking has advantages in times of imminent danger, as a situation is reduced to simplest considerations to allow a rapid decision and potentially life-saving response. This may have been a necessity in evolutionary times past, and on occasion today. However, across the broader spectrum of human activity, it often engenders a false sense of urgency about a situation and pressures one into discounting options which do not drive toward a resolution in a short time frame. Mutual interests and considerations of common ground are ignored or viewed with skepticism by this reasoning. Where resources are in great supply a system can abide this type of behavior in a limited arena. On an even playing field and within limited confines it has served to define the rules of conduct which allow parties to a dispute to arrive at ostensibly fair short-term resolutions. (e.g.: sporting events). The adversarial linear perspective has often provided short term gains for one party in an encounter. In the case of Man vs. Nature, the gains for Man have admittedly been localized and short term. What happens is that the future is trashed.

The adversarial perspective results in sacrifice of the well-being of future generations (and possibly the future of current generations) on the altar of instant gratification. According to this perspective our children, who are our future, are viewed as adversaries to the indulgences of the present. The only long term winners in an adversarial encounter, be it on a global scale or more locally in an economic or political or legal realm, are the arbiters of the dispute. It is usually the case that both parties to the dispute in the long run are harmed. In Man vs. Nature, the arbiters may be simpler life forms such as viruses, bacteria, or parasites.

The linear viewpoint limits our perspective to proximate influences and consequences of actions. This is analogous to viewing reality as two dimensional rather than three dimensional. Also, linear thinking discounts future time as a measure of importance, particularly in its avoidance of long-term consequences of current decisions and actions.

Taken together, the adversarial culture and linear analysis have combined to provide the lens through which reality is viewed. This type of thinking has been to a large degree encoded in our legal system and defines, by law, how we must behave towards each other. It is epitomized in such phrases as "survival of the fittest," "let the buyer beware" and "looking out for number one." It manifests itself in concepts such as the feeling "if you're not 100% for me, then you're against me." This framework has allowed us to advance two general approaches to current problems of environmental deterioration.

One approach is to eliminate entirely an identified danger. This approach has been used with respect to substances such as DDT and lead. While the results of the elimination approach have shown measurable successes in reducing exposure to targeted environmental hazards, there are many who feel that the costs of generalizing this approach to all risk factors outweigh the advantages. Such an approach may in fact detract from our ability to solve other problems which may be as serious or more serious than the individual problems targeted. A case in point is the acknowledged problem of lead exposure among children. This has received in some areas remarkably effective (e.g., lead-free gasoline) and other areas marginally effective efforts to reduce exposure to environmental lead. Everyone agrees that high levels of exposure need immediate attention. There has even been some evidence to show that measurable decreases in low level lead exposure can result in marginal but measurable correlative increases in IQ testing. While this is a worthy goal, it can be quite expensive and sometimes when applied to children who are in low-level ranges of exposure diverts resources that might otherwise be used for efforts such as nutritional supplementation, vaccinations, or educational efforts. Programs of these latter types may, in the long run, be more important to the individuals affected, and possibly more effective at promoting general health and well being, including improving IQ test results.

This is not to recommend that nothing be done about low-level exposure to hazardous substances, nor is this information meant to detract from the often noble motives which have resulted in such efforts. Furthermore it is appropriate that we share a sense of urgency in lowering exposures which are of immediate and overwhelming danger, and we should always seek to minimize or eliminate hazardous exposures. However, we need to remain mindful of the fact that we have limited resources with which to work and prioritizing the use of those resources in addressing existing hazards is an important consideration when dealing with levels of exposure to substances in ranges of non-vital consequences.

The second approach is the concept of controlling or reducing waste production and pollution. This is the more widely applied concept in use. We see this in efforts at recycling, increasing the efficiency and cleanliness of production processes, partially destroying wastes (incineration), storing wastes (landfilling), and economic sanctions against certain categories of pollutants (selling sulfur dioxide emission warrants to utility and industry sources).

One of the battlegrounds in this arena is **waste incineration.** Large corporations and many municipalities have committed to this form of waste reduction. There currently exist several incineration technologies. One of these is the cement kiln, which uses hazardous waste as fuel supplement to generate heat for the production of cement. Other furnace technologies are also employed in incineration. It is generally believed that the various incineration technologies reduce the volume of wastes by 70 to 90%. However, the residual ash may contain increased concentrations of hazardous materials including dioxans and heavy metals. Evidence suggests that dioxans are actually produced by the process of incineration in some kilns. The residual ash presents another disposal problem which is yet to be solved in an effective and agreeable manner. Some jurisdictions have chosen to reclassify the residual ash as other than hazardous to lessen the costs and complexities of dealing with its disposal. This has been labeled "linguistic detoxification." Similarly many household wastes and some industrial wastes, which would be hazardous by objective evaluation, are exempted from this classification as we continue to dump potentially hazardous materials into municipal sewage systems. Tremendous energy and creativity have been employed in the political arena to obtain special classifications for such waste materials. These creative energies would be better directed toward finding solutions to the underlying problems. This misdirected effort is a result of the process of adversarial linear thinking.

Landfilling is another classic example of an adversarial linear approach to wastes. As we generate solid wastes at an accelerating rate we have achieved a new standard to measure human construction. It is generally acknowledged that the largest structure ever created by mankind is a solid municipal waste dump (landfill). This is testament to the current state of human technologies of production and consumption, and highlights our need to rearrange our priorities.

Sometimes euphemistically referred to as "sanitary landfills," landfills are serving as a temporary reservoir for solid and sometimes liquid wastes. There are currently estimated to be some five thousand open municipal landfills in the United States. Over 20,000 have been retired from operation. These are divided into two basic types, wet and dry. **Dry landfills** are the most widely used. These attempt to isolate the materials placed in the landfill from air and moisture. This prevents rotting and biodegradation. At first glance this has the attraction of taking waste products and keeping them out of sight and circulation. However, the substances placed in these landfills persist and will ultimately need to be addressed. On the other hand, **wet landfills** result in accelerated biodegradation with increased production of methane and liquid effluents, so-called leachate. The half-life of the substances contained in such a landfill is much shorter than that in a dry landfill, but the problems of dealing with methane which potentially is explosive, and with leachate which can contain hazardous materials depending upon the substances in the landfill, have yet to be adequately addressed. There are efforts underway to utilize the methane as a source of energy, and to control the leachate through improved site linings. However, the problems associated with these efforts remain substantial. Moreover, much of the bulk of wastes remain, and in many instances, the half-life of dangerous substances present in the landfill is much longer than the guaranteed safety of the landfill itself. Landfills often contain hazardous substances unknown to the general public or even to the trustees and administrators of the landfills. This results from unwitting and sometimes deliberate deposits of such materials at these sites.

On a local level with a stable population waste reduction efforts decrease the rate at which pressures are put on the environment. However, when viewed from a broader perspective and taking the tremendous overall growth in the world's population into account along with the huge amounts of waste which have already been generated, this approach is guaranteed to add to current problems. The net effect is one of an inexorable march toward a future which cannot sustain the quality of life as we know it. This information is not meant to detract from the efforts which are underway and which may be in and of themselves worthy of pursuit and improvement. But this information underscores the need to bring about a fundamental change in our approach to the problems of environmental degradation.

For one thing, we need to rid ourselves of the "throw away society" mentality which is an outgrowth of adversarial linear thinking. This has permeated our lives and is destroying not only our environment, but social institutions and family values as well. While concepts of recycling and waste reduction will justifiably continue to be pursued, no amount of individual or household waste reduction or recycling can offset the overall increases in waste production which will attend the expansion of current technologies and the burgeoning worldwide population.

A classic example of an adversarial linear approach to an environmental problem is **phytoremediation.** This is an attempt to develop plants which can selectively take up heavy metals from soils and incorporate them in plant substance. Disposal of the plant substance becomes a new problem substituting for the soil contamination. Accelerated biologic concentration of these toxic metals is a possible result. This approach does not solve the underlying problem, but seeks only to address a symptom (heavy metal contamination of soil) of a more fundamental systemic disorder.

In the search for increasing yields, strains of **pesticide-resistant crops** are being developed. While this may allow greater yields in those areas treated with such chemicals, debate exists over the soundness of this approach to farming as it encourages the continued and even enhanced use of pesticides, which in turn have harmful effects on the ecosystem. This represents another classic example of ameliorating a symptom of a more fundamental disorder. The possibility of net worsening of the general condition of the environment through applications of these types of efforts signals the danger in adversarial linear approaches to environmental problems.

For the immediate future we are limited by adversarial linear thinking to these two general approaches. 1. Elimination of those substances which are most hazardous and amenable to elimination and; 2. Reduction or controlling the majority of our waste production, including landfilling and incineration.

There has been a growing call for a new approach to thinking about these problems. In many respects this summons represents a return to basic principles in the sense that we have now recognized that our long term survival as a species and the preservation of an hospitable biosphere depend on a keen awareness of the complete interdependency of mankind and all of the elements in our environment, and that we are a part of and dependent upon Nature.

THE COOPERATIVE SYSTEMS PARADIGM

The Man vs. Nature adversarial linear perspective which has dominated our thought processes is now recognized as a faulty perspective from which to view our relationship with Nature. We are trapped in a scenario described as the "tragedy of the commons" by systems analysts. That is, we have limited resources in the biosphere upon which all life forms are critically interdependent and no one life form can disproportionately use and abuse these resources without harming the ecosystem and eventually harming itself. We have stressed the biosphere in diverse ways using an adversarial linear perspective which includes a distorted proximate focus and skewed cost-benefits analysis in industry and technology. While efforts based on this fundamentally flawed perspective have resulted in short term gains for local or regional communities, it is clear that the net effect has been a negative impact on the biosphere and a serious threat to life as we know it. Furthermore, this mental construct (paradigm) restricts our ability to redress existing damage to the environment. It limits our options to the types of approaches outlined above, proffering short term, local solutions of convenience while failing to address the underlying problems. It is largely symptoms and not causes which are approached by this type of thinking. We know that Man and Nature coexist, inextricably interdependent, in the process of life on this planet. We have recognized the need to accept this philosophic viewpoint, now we need to translate this viewpoint into thought processes which not only reflect this reality, but will also dominate our economic, technological, legal and political thinking.

A developing body of knowledge in management theory centers upon **"systems thinking."** Cooperative systems thinking is an articulation in management circles of the wisdom of our ancestors in recognizing the need for cooperation and of our interdependence. It recognizes the fallacies and weaknesses of adversarial linear categorizations as matters of convenience which only serve to cloud the issues of reality to gain short-term advantages at the expense of long term strategic well-being. Systems thinking focuses on processes and seeks a complete perspective from which to assess a problem. On the other hand, linear thinking focuses on events which are often symptoms of more fundamental problems, while discounting remote influences and consequences, and failing to see the processes which give rise to the symptoms.

Cooperative systems thinking places a priority on factoring in the total consequences, both proximate and remote of decisions and actions. Additionally, it is based on a foundation of ethical and objective evaluation of current conditions. Systems thinking itself is not new. It is paraphrased by such basic concepts as "know thyself" and "accepting responsibility for one's actions," admonitions such as "be careful what you wish for because you may be granted your wish," and statements such as "what goes around, comes around." What is new is that this systems approach is being articulated in a manner that targets individuals in positions of decision making and political power. Policy makers are being made aware that these fundamental values can be applied profitably at all levels of human endeavor including directing means of production and influencing patterns of consumption. By placing priority on the total consequences of actions we will defer short term gains to long range strategic well-being. In the environmental arena it may be that we face the most serious long term consequences of the flawed logic of adversarial linear thinking. Non-adversarial systems concepts may change the way in which economists calculate costs of production by utilizing the concept of Total Cost Accounting. This requires factoring in the costs of natural resource depletion and environmental damage when determining an item's cost. Such an accounting system may allow us to see the advantages of environmentally benign technologies, which may at first glance look to cost more; however, when the full costs of resource depletion and environmental restoration are included, environmentally benign technologies are often more cost effective than current technologies.

A recently espoused **theory of criticality** is a corollary of system's thinking. It describes how small changes through cumulative systemic effects can have widespread consequences. Two analogies of how small, seemingly isolated insults can have widespread or perhaps even global consequences are offered. If one takes the concept of a sand pile being produced by successive addition of grains of sand dropping on a pile, it is observed that there are times when the pile reaches a point at which the addition of a single extra grain of sand results in a small avalanche. Also, there are times at which that pile reaches a state that the addition of a single grain results in a large avalanche transforming the entire pile. That last grain of sand was not inherently different from any other. It simply impacted at a critical point. In a chemis-try lab a similar phenomenon can be observed in acid-base experiments wherein the color of a solution is monitored with sequential addition of drops of an acid or base. The solution remains the same color throughout the sequence of additional drops until a point is reached in the solution wherein the addition of one single drop dramatically changes not only the color, but also the nature of the large container of fluid. This signifies the point at which the buffering capacity of the system has been stretched beyond its limits. That last drop of fluid was inherently no different than any other. It simply impacted at a critical point.

In a manner similar to these examples, "sand drops" of environmental degradation are occurring throughout the world in seemingly small but assuredly cumulative events. We have perhaps already reached stages of criticality in which additional small, apparently localized insults to the environment will result in widespread changes of tremendous magnitude. These changes may be irreversible, the results unfavorable.

A rapid growth in understanding of total quality concepts and systems thinking is occurring in management circles. Hopefully this understanding will be reflected in a change in the ways in which we produce and consume goods and services. Intensive germinal efforts are underway to change some of the most environmentally abusive technologies. Environmentally benign technologies are gaining acceptance in concept. Given mankind's abilities to adapt and innovate, it is reasonable to expect that large scale efforts can result in new processes for chemical synthesis that will sustain a balance between human interests and environmental quality. In agriculture, organic farming is a systems approach to the problems which agriculture brings to bear on the biosphere. Employing solar and geothermal energy sources represent systems approaches to energy production which are more environmentally sound than fossil fuels or nuclear energy. Efforts at reforestation, even the planting and nurturing of individual trees, represent attempts to correct a fundamental problem and serve as examples of how a systems approach can be participated in by individuals and households, and should be a high priority for industries and governments. Mass transit and human powered as well as electric powered vehicles represent systems approaches to transportation. Total Cost Accounting, if required by law, would represent a legal/economic application of systems thought that could shift the focus of new technologies toward the environmentally benign portion of the spectrum of technology. Taken together, such approaches show that the possibility of a global technological transformation towards a sustainable biosphere is within our reach, and that there is a role for individuals and households as well as industries and nations in this effort.

Cooperative systems thinking needs to be embraced at corporate board levels and espoused in our educational institutions and law schools. Not only the captains of industry, but also those who encode our values in the form of laws, regulations and judicial decrees, need to embrace this concept of systems responsibility if we are to have hope of saving our biosphere. This means reversing a century or two of adversarial culture which has permeated and dominated our social, political, economic, and legal arenas. A **paradigm shift** is called for in our attitudes and activities as they relate to the environment and as we relate toward each other. We must **replace adversarial with cooperative culture** and **replace linear with systems analysis.** A cooperative systems approach will be the foundation upon which mankind can make peace with the environment and re-establish the balances in nature which over the long run best serve the interests of life on this planet.

The Hope of Trillium

The Trillium Trail symbolizes the path of hope we can follow to preserve the balanced quality that Nature provides. The concept of **balance** permeates throughout Nature. Balance is incorporated by many ethicists as a critical component of ethical behavior. Often balance is manifest in cycles which are not readily apparent to the casual observer of a snapshot in time. We need to realize that cycles are integral to the balance of Nature and to gain an appreciation for our place on this planet through firsthand experience of the cyclical beauty and wonders of Nature.

Communing with Nature offers an insight that strikes the senses and impacts the psyche in a manner which cannot be fully conveyed in language. Those who have internalized a respect for Nature's beauty and balance generally feel a heightened sense of stewardship toward our planet and an admiration for all of the interrelated entities which make up our biosphere. We are all inextricably connected with every life form on this planet. We are composed of atoms and molecules which make their way through the biosphere, being borrowed by us for what amount to very short periods before being recycled into the environment. As Pamela reminds us in her poem, **"Every drop of water, every breath of air, every ray of sunshine is part of what we share"** and will continue to be shared with all life forms throughout the biosphere for as long as life exists.

In Native American lore, the spider web has been used to illustrate the interconnectedness of man and the environment. Any event that occurs anywhere in the web reverberates throughout the entirety of the web. In a similar fashion, all of the insults that we lay upon the environment will reverberate throughout the biosphere.

We need to understand that labeling something as "progress" does not necessarily make it so. Just as linguistic detoxification does not render a substance less hazardous, the designation of something as "progress" is not a proof of progress. **Progress** really implies an improvement in the quality of life, not for the short term or for a segment of the population, but rather for the long term and across the broad spectrum of humanity. Such progress will not result from the license to consume and dispose of natural resources in haphazard or self-serving ways, but rather will be achieved through discipline which recognizes unwritten laws of cooperation and rejects the acquisitiveness of adversarial linear perspectives. Recognizing that we have system wide responsibilities and de-emphasizing our rights as they have come to be understood through an adversarial lens will be necessary to achieving true progress.

Thinking in terms of cooperative systems is a challenge facing our policy makers and those who control the means of production and transportation. Industrial waste dwarfs household waste by a factor of at least 50 to one. While efforts on an individual and household level are worthy, it is at the level of corporate and governmental decision-making where the greatest leverage for environmental improvement exists. In the long term it is only through recognition of our interconnectedness that we can avoid arriving at a critical state wherein even small additional changes can wreak havoc on our environment, and upon ourselves.

While individuals need to further the efforts of families, communities, and nations in terms of reducing wastes and recycling, more importantly we need to encourage development of environmentally benign technologies and changes in our methodologies of transportation and patterns of consumption. We need to move toward more environmentally sound practices across the spectrum of human activities. Assuming stewardship responsibilities toward our planet at every level of human endeavor will help secure a future for our children and grandchildren and for their children and grandchildren. We should not sacrifice the environmental inheritance of future generations on the altar of the false god of "progress," to which too much has already been sacrificed.

Through the unbalanced approach toward our environment of the past century, we have threatened species of animals and plants to a degree unseen since the birth of civilization. In so doing, we have threatened the quality of human existence. The philosophic foundation of the answer to our current problems is not new. The wisdom of the ancients speaks to us about such things as balance, moderation, harmony and respect for the Earth.

We need to become more aware, through education, of the total consequences of our actions. We need to commit ourselves to caring about our environment, realizing that we live on what amounts to a fragile veneer on the Earth constituting the biosphere. Finally, we need to develop a willingness to recognize and accept the changes in thinking which will be necessary for adapting our technological, economic, political, and legal efforts to allow repair of the damage which has been wrought upon the biosphere, and then to sustain Nature's delicate balances.

The Trillium flower is a symbol of modest beauty. This is a notion which has been overlooked in our age of instant gratification and glamorous consumption. Modest beauty itself is a concept that we would do well to revisit and nourish. This includes respect for the beauty of all of Nature's creations, respect for ourselves and for each other. This respect will help us to become educated to the risks of our behaviors, to commit ourselves to the duties we have toward each other and toward our environment, and to devote energies and creativity to repairing the damage which has been done and to preventing future irreparable harm to our biosphere. This is the Trillium Trail which we invite you to travel.